How many people does it take to make a difference?

ACKNOWLEDGEMENTS

The quotations in this book were gathered lovingly but unscientifically over several years and/or were contributed by many friends or acquaintances. Some arrived – and survived in our files – on scraps of paper and may therefore be imperfectly worded or attributed. To the authors, contributors and original sources, our thanks, and where appropriate, our apologies. ~The Editors

WITH SPECIAL THANKS TO

Jason Aldrich, Gerry Baird, Jay Baird, Neil Beaton, Josie Bissett, Laura Boro, Jim and Alyssa Darragh & Family, Marta and Kyle Drevniak, Jennifer and Matt Ellison & Family, Rob Estes, Michael and Leianne Flynn & Family, Sarah Forster, Jennifer Hurwitz, Heidi Jones, Carol Anne Kennedy, June Martin, Jessica Phoenix and Tom DesLongchamp, Janet Potter & Family, Diane Roger, Kirsten and Garrett Sessions, Andrea Shirley, Lin Smith, Clarie Yam and Erik Lee, Heidi Yamada & Family, Justi and Tote Yamada & Family, Bob and Val Yamada, Kaz and Kristin Yamada & Family, Tai and Joy Yamada, Anne Zadra, August and Arline Zadra, and Gus and Rosie Zadra.

Credits

Written by Dan Zadra and Kobi Yamada; Edited by Kristel Wills; Designed by Steve Potter

ISBN 978-1-932319-72-9

1st Printing. 20K 03 09
Printed in China

WHAT DOES A GREAT LIFE LOOK LIKE?

ASK A HUNDRED PEOPLE WHAT A GREAT LIFE LOOKS LIKE AND YOU'LL PROBABLY GET A HUNDRED DIFFERENT ANSWERS—BUT CERTAIN ANSWERS WILL MAKE VIRTUALLY EVERYONE'S LIST.

MOST PEOPLE WOULD AGREE, FOR EXAMPLE, THAT A GREAT LIFE INCLUDES SOMETHING WORTH LIVING FOR, MAYBE EVEN WORTH DYING FOR. A PORTION OF A GREAT LIFE WOULD BE DEVOTED TO SOMETHING BIGGER, GREATER, GRANDER THAN YOURSELF. SOMETHING THAT INSPIRES YOU, ENERGIZES YOU, PULLS YOU FORWARD. SOMETHING THAT RESPONDS TO YOUR UNIQUE TALENT OR TOUCH AND, ULTIMATELY, MAKES A DIFFERENCE IN THE WORLD AROUND YOU.

A GREAT LIFE WOULD NATURALLY BRING MORE MEANING, PURPOSE, LOVE, LAUGHTER, WONDER AND ADVENTURE TO YOUR DAYS. AND, AT THE END OF YOUR JOURNEY YOU WOULD LOOK BACK ON A LIFE OF SIGNIFICANCE, RATHER THAN REGRET—KNOWING IN YOUR HEART THAT YOU LEFT THE WORLD BETTER THAN YOU FOUND IT. KNOWING THAT YOU MADE A DIFFERENCE IN THE LIVES OF OTHERS. KNOWING THAT YOU GOT SOMETHING WONDERFUL OUT OF IT, AND YOU GAVE SOMETHING WONDERFUL BACK.

A GREAT LIFE, OF COURSE, IS NOT SOMETHING WE EXPERIENCE, IT'S SOMETHING WE CREATE. THAT'S WHAT THIS BOOK IS ALL ABOUT.

How many people
does it take to
make a difference?

One

One song can spark a moment
One flower can wake the dream
One tree can start a forest
One bird can herald spring
One smile begins a friendship
One handclasp lifts a soul

One star can guide a ship at sea
One word can frame the goal
One vote can change a nation
One sunbeam lights a room
One candle wipes out darkness
One laugh will conquer gloom
One step must start each journey
One word must start a prayer
One hope will raise our spirits
One touch can show you care
One voice can speak with wisdom
One heart can know what's true
One life can make a difference
That difference starts with you.

~Unknown

The world needs more you in it.

In her speeches, Marian Wright Edelman, founder of the Children's Defense Fund, reminds us that a lot of people these days are still waiting for Martin Luther King, Jr., Mother Teresa or Mahatma Gandhi to come back—but they are gone. We are it. It is up to us now. It is up to you. More than ever before, our world needs more goodness, more kindness, more caring, more action, more "you" in it.

John F. Kennedy said that one person can make a difference, and every person must try. What if each of us really tried? What if each of us spontaneously decided that, one by one, we really can be the better world we wish for?

This is our time,
yours and mine.

You have important discoveries to make.
Now is the time to make them.

You have important talents to develop.
Now is the time to develop them.

You have important gifts to give to the world.
Now is the time to give them.

Tell me, what is it you plan to do
with your one wild and precious life?

~Mary Oliver

For hundreds of years, philosophers, artists, teachers, mystics and poets have celebrated the endless possibilities of the human spirit. But none more eloquently than the brilliant Spanish composer Pablo Casals.

Casals wrote that his music sprang "directly from his awareness of the wonder of life and the joy of feeling the incredible marvel of being a human being." And he urged us to start seeing our own possibilities and those of our children in the bright light of mutual compassion:

YOU ARE A MARVEL

"When will we teach our children in school what they are? We should say to each of them: Do you know what you are? You are a marvel. You are unique. In all of the world there is no other child exactly like you. In the millions of years that have passed there has never been another child like you.

"And look at your body—what a wonder it is! Your legs, your arms, your cunning fingers, the way you move! You may become a Shakespeare, a Michelangelo, a Beethoven. You have the capacity for anything.

"Yes, you are a marvel. And when you grow up, can you then harm another who, like you, is a marvel?"

If we have never been amazed by the very fact that we exist,
we are squandering the greatest fact of all. ~Will Durant

Statistically, the probability of any one of us being born exactly as we are in this precise time and place is so unlikely that your very existence verges on the miraculous and should be a continuing source of dazzlement for you.

Odds of bowling a 300 game: 1 in 11,500

ODDS

Odds of being hit by lightning: 1 in 576,000

OF

Odds of getting a royal flush on your first five cards: 1 in 649,740

YOUR

Odds of becoming U.S. President: 1 in 10,000,000

BEING

Odds of winning $340 million jackpot in MegaMillions lottery: about 1 in 175,000,000

BORN

Odds of your being born in this particular time, place and circumstance: about 1 in 400,000,000,000 **

** Odds calculated by factoring in the chances of survival of a continuous lineage of more than 100,000 generations of your predecessors, all surviving successive natural disasters throughout more than a million years of geological time, including factors of evolution, biogenesis, specific sperm and egg combinations, ultimately merging successfully together to result in the one-and-only YOU.

You are not here by mistake.

Around the world and down through the ages there has never been another you, and there will never be another you. The miracle of your existence is now in your hands. You are here for a purpose. You have something that only you can give to the world. Take time to consider what that is.

It is paradoxical but profoundly true that the most certain way for people to bring hope, help, meaning and joy to their own lives is by reaching out and bringing hope, help, meaning and joy to the lives of others. If you've already experienced this beautiful phenomenon for yourself, you are in good company.

Martin Luther King, Jr., Civil Rights leader: *"Life's most persistent and urgent question is: What are you doing for others?"*

Albert Einstein, physicist: *"Each of us is here for a brief sojourn; for what purpose we know not, though sometimes we sense it. But we know from daily life that we exist for other people first of all, for whose smiles and well-being our own happiness depends."*

Danny Thomas, founder, St. Jude's Hospital: *"All of us are born for a reason, but all of us don't discover why. Success in life has nothing to do with what you gain in life or accomplish for yourself. It's what you do for others."*

Ralph Waldo Emerson, poet: *"Unselfish acts are the real miracles out of which all the reported miracles grow."*

Robert Ingersoll, scholar: *"We rise by lifting others."*

Margaret Mead, anthropologist: *"I must admit that I personally measure success in terms of the contributions an individual makes to her or his fellow human beings."*

Albert Schweitzer, humanitarian: *"I don't know what your destiny will be, but this I know: the only ones among you who will be truly happy are those who will have sought and found how to serve."*

Ask Yourself:

WHO AM I?

WHY AM I HERE?

WHAT AM I DOING FOR OTHERS?

Seattle is a beautiful place, but in the 1980s I was living in a beat-up beach cabin. I had an old TV, a lumpy futon, and one of those white plastic Princess phones. I was basically broke, but my noisy old refrigerator was stuffed with fresh vegetables, eggs, fruit, beer and frozen pizza—and I had a spectacular view of Puget Sound, the Olympic Mountains and the Seattle skyline.

That year, I volunteered to host a college exchange student from Guinea-Bissau, Africa. When I picked him up at the airport, Salvatore was easy to spot. He was 23, tall and regal-looking, with a huge smile and lustrous blue-black skin. He had lived his entire life as a barefoot fisherman in a small native village located on a big river deep in the jungle of Guinea-Bissau—and now his village had raised the money to send him to study U.S. Fisheries on their behalf. He had travelled directly from his African village to Seattle, and I could see he was astonished at what he saw as we drove through the beautiful city.

When we arrived at my raggedy cabin, I worried that Salvatore might be disappointed with his new accommodations. He seemed somber as I showed him the little bedroom, bathroom, kitchen, TV and telephone. What was Salvatore thinking? I decided to take him out on the little deck to try to impress him with the view. The snow-clad mountains were spread out against the sky that day, and one of Seattle's majestic white ferries was gliding across the sparkling waters of Puget Sound. We stood there silently for awhile, and then Salvatore turned to me with his brow deeply knit in thought.

"You are a king?" he asked. "No," I laughed, "I'm just an everyday person like you." Salvatore was silent for a moment, and then he turned again and said quite clearly and emphatically, "You are a king." And it suddenly dawned on me that he was right. All these years I had been a king and not known it.

By Scott Sabol, Ph.D.

SO, WHO ARE YOU REALLY?

YOU ARE ROYALTY

If you have food in your refrigerator, clothes on your back, a roof overhead and a place to sleep…you are richer than 75% of the world's population.

If you have a little money in the bank or spare change in a dish someplace… you are among the top 8% of the world's wealthy.

If you can drink from your kitchen faucet whenever you want…you are more fortunate by far than 1.5 billion people who have no access to clean water at all.

If you can attend a church or a political rally without fear of harassment, arrest, torture or death…you have the kind of freedom denied to more than three billion people in the world.

If you can read this message, you are more blessed than two billion people who cannot read at all.

If your everyday problems are weighing you down, there are millions of people on Earth who would gladly trade places with you right now—problems and all—and feel they have been royally blessed.

Remember: "From those to whom much is given, much is expected."

What does hope feel like? What does courage sound like?

What does action look like? How do things get better?

All of you reading these words

have loved someone,

have done someone a kindness,

have healed a wound,

have taken on a challenge,

have created something beautiful,

and have enjoyed breathing the air of existence

Every moment you make a difference.

~Random Acts of Kindness

YOU'RE ALREADY MAKING A DIFFERENCE

One of the greatest misconceptions that people live in is that they don't really impact the lives of others.

Volunteers who work with tough inner-city gang members can dispel this misconception in a few minutes through a powerful ritual called "strength bombardment." Basically, one gang member stands silently in the center of the gang, while the other members take turns telling him a) what they think his unique strengths are, and b) how he has impacted each of them in positive ways. It is not unusual to see even the toughest gang members break down and cry when they hear what their peers actually think of them.

It's exciting and moving for all of us (not just gang members) to discover the power for good that we possess and have been exercising without even knowing it. You've touched people and known it. You've also touched people and may never know it.

Julia Butterfly Hill, the American environmentalist, wrote, "The question is not 'Can you make a difference?' You already do make a difference. It's just a matter of what kind of difference you want to make, during your life on this planet."

Your life can be a path of coincidence, happenstance, and luck, or it can be a purposefully charted course to touch the lives of others and make the differences that only you can make in the world.

Begin Charting Your Course

IN MY LIFE SO FAR...

Someone I've already taught or mentored:

Someone I've already supported or helped:

Someone I've already encouraged or inspired:

Someone I've already forgiven:

Something in my community I've already changed for the better:

MOVING FORWARD...

Someone I will teach or mentor:

Someone I will support or help:

Someone I will encourage or inspire:

Someone I will forgive:

Something in my community I will change for the better:

I'm asking you to believe. Not just in my ability to bring about real change... I'm asking you to believe in yours.

~Barack Obama

The start to a better world is our belief that it is possible.

Believe in your dreams.

Believe in today.

Believe that you are loved.

Believe that you make a difference.

Believe we can build a better world.

Believe when others might not.

Believe there's a light at the end of the tunnel.

Believe that you might be that light for someone else.

Believe that the best is yet to be.

Believe in each other.

Believe in yourself.

I believe in you.

~Kobi Yamada

Will Tough Times Pull Us Together... Or Pull Us Apart?

During difficult times, some say that people will think only of themselves—that it's every man for himself—but is that really the case?

In the midst of the mortgage meltdown and financial crisis, Nancy Gibbs of *Time Magazine* wrote that there seems to be another kind of story at large in our land. It's the story of millions of people who believe that problems shared grow smaller, that courage is contagious, that each of us can make a difference in the lives of our neighbors, and that a crisis is an opportunity to pull together instead of pulling apart:

- Someone placed an 18-karat-gold diamond ring in the Salvation Army kettle in Uniontown, Pennsylvania.

- Food donations in Paradise, California are up five-fold.

- A Santa Clarita, California family took in an 83-year-old woman left homeless by wildfires and helped rebuild her life.

- A Sioux Falls, South Dakota hotel manager came up with a plan to open his doors to 200 homeless people at Christmas.

- Mississippi, which ranks as the poorest state, is also the most generous in charitable giving.

Maybe as times get worse we get better. Our pain makes us feel other people's too; our fear lets us practice valor; we are tense, and tender as well. And among the things we can no longer afford are things we never really wanted anyway....

~Nancy Gibbs

HEROES

RE EXTRAORDINARY TO SOMEONE TOO. —*Helen Hayes*

Those who say there are no heroes left in the world just don't know where to look. You can see heroes every day, going in and out of schools, hospitals, homes and businesses.

Heroes are everyday people who have chosen to give a portion of their lives to something bigger than themselves. Heroes light a candle in the dark. They just have a way of brightening our world with a word, an example, a gift, a hand, an idea.

We all need heroes. They inspire us to be better versions of ourselves.

Who are your heroes and how do they inspire you?

....
....
....
....

What more could you be doing to encourage, help, support or inspire those who look up to you?

....
....
....
....

To the world you may be one person, but to one person you may be the world. ~ Josephine Billings

Go ahead and cry, I'll catch your tears…A few weeks after one of his classmates died, an eight-year-old boy decided to visit the classmate's home one day after school. Later when he returned home, his mother was surprised to find out where the boy had been. "What did you say?" she asked him gently. "Nothing," he replied. "I just sat on his mom's lap and helped her cry."

You never know how much good a simple smile can do…Each morning a middle school teacher noticed a lone student standing out in the hallway. The boy had a withered arm and leg, and he always stood unsmiling and alone. None of the other students spoke with him. The teacher decided to make a point of greeting the boy in the hall each morning with a friendly smile and hello. On the last day of school, the teacher found a bright yellow envelope on his desk. Inside was a note from the student. All it said was, "Dear Mr. Tice, it was so nice of you to say hello to me in the hall each day."

Even your mere presence can be a present to the world…There once was an elderly, despondent woman in a nursing home. She wouldn't speak to anyone or request anything. She merely existed—rocking the day away in her rocking chair. The old woman didn't have many visitors, but every couple of mornings a concerned young nurse would go into her room. The nurse didn't try to speak or ask questions. She simply pulled up another rocking chair beside the old woman and rocked with her. Weeks later, the old woman finally spoke. There were tears in her eyes. "Thank you," she said, "for rocking with me."

Today, will you stop to help someone in need, or will you turn away?

Which path of service is yours?

There is a cause or an issue out there with your name on it, something you care about, someplace where you can serve or make a difference in a way that is unique to you. Whatever it is, find it—and follow it. Let the answers to these questions guide you.

List Your Concerns

To make a difference is not a matter of accident, a matter of casual occurrence of the tides. People choose to make a difference.

~Maya Angelou

Causes I care about—things that get my creative juices flowing:

Things that upset me, or make my blood boil:

Things that make me sad, cry or feel indignant:

Issues I always talk about with my friends:

Are you a "natural" at entertaining children, working with animals, giving speeches, planning events, taking pictures, talking on the phone, being patient with the elderly, crunching numbers, writing letters, rallying support...or just working quietly behind the scenes to get things done?

Know in your heart that these gifts are given to you for a reason—how can you use them for good? Just draw lines to connect your concerns with your strengths.

List Your Strengths

Things I am good at:

Things that make me feel good:

Talents I would be excited to use more:

My unique background or experience:

Everybody has a strength to share. If we can tap into that—if people can find ways to contribute whatever their particular unique talent or gift is, then that really can change the world.

~Bill Shore, founder, Share Our Strength

do good.

Help publicly. Help privately. Help in your actions by recycling and conserving and protecting, but help also in your attitude. Help make sense where sense has gone missing. Help bring reason and respect to discourse and debate. Help science to solve and faith to soothe. Help law bring justice, until justice is commonplace. Help and you will abolish apathy—the void that is so quickly filled by ignorance and evil. ~Tom Hanks

Harvard's Most Famous Dropout Delivers a College Commencement Speech

Bill Gates dropped out of Harvard in his junior year before co-founding Microsoft and going on to become the world's richest person. In 2007, Gates went back to Harvard to collect an honorary law degree and deliver the commencement address. His message (shown in part at right) was both an inspiration and a challenge:

Members of the Harvard Family: Here in the Yard this afternoon is one of the great collections of intellectual talent in the world. What for? When you consider what those of us here in this Yard have been given—in talent, privilege and opportunity—there is almost no limit to what the world has a right to expect from us. You graduates are coming of age in an amazing time. As you leave school, you have technology that members of my class never had. You have awareness of global inequity, which we did not have. And I hope you will come back here to Harvard 30 years from now and reflect on what you have done with your talent and your energy. I hope you will judge yourselves not on your professional accomplishments alone, but also on how well you have addressed the world's deepest inequities...on how well you treated people a world away who have nothing in common with you but their humanity.

~Bill Gates

LOOK OUT OVER THE NEXT
10
20
30
YEARS OF YOUR LIFE.

What are the most important things you are going to devote your time and energy to—your highest callings?

....

....

....

....

....

....

....

....

How will you personally help address the world's deepest inequities?

....

....

....

....

....

....

....

....

....

Who is the most important person in the organization?

Everyone.

In his book, *Teaching the Elephant to Dance,* author Jim Belasco tells the story of Dr. Denton Cooley, the famous heart surgeon.

One day Belasco followed Dr. Cooley on his rounds and, en route to the operating room, saw the surgeon stop and talk to a man mopping the hallway. The two men conversed for nearly ten minutes before Dr. Cooley dashed into the operating room. Curious, Belasco walked over to the man with the mop and said, "That was a long conversation."

The man replied, "Yes, Dr. Cooley and I talk quite often."

Then Belasco asked, "What exactly do you do at the hospital?"

The man replied, "We save lives."

In the best organizations, there is no such thing as them and us; there is only "we"—all of us working together. In the big picture everyone has a unique role to fill…everyone has a piece to the puzzle…everyone, including and perhaps especially *you*, makes a difference.

What is my job?

What about my job really counts?

How well am I doing?

Is my job an expression of my personal values?

In my job, am I building a life of success, but not of significance?

What can I (and/or my employer) do to help me become more passionate about my current role?

Is there another job I would rather be doing?

Why aren't I doing it?

Less than 20 percent of Americans can answer these with any clarity.
(Guess which 20 percent.)

Your work is going to fill a large part of your life, and the only way to be truly satisfied is to do what you believe is great work. And the only way to do great work is to love what you do. If you haven't found it yet, keep looking. Don't settle. Stay hungry. Stay foolish. ~Steve Jobs

DON'T BE BEATEN DOWN BY NAYSAYERS.

THEY'LL CALL YOU A DREAMER, A DO-GOODER OR A ROMANTIC. EVERY TIME YOU STAND UP FOR A GOOD CAUSE—LARGE OR SMALL—SOMEONE WILL ROLL THEIR EYES OR TELL YOU TO SIT BACK DOWN. ROBERT KENNEDY USED TO SAY THAT 20 PERCENT OF THE PEOPLE ARE AGAINST EVERYTHING ALL THE TIME. IT'S TRUE. THERE WILL ALWAYS BE LOTS OF PEOPLE WHO CAN GIVE YOU ALL THE REASONS WHY YOU CAN'T OR WON'T IMPROVE THE WORLD. IT'S UP TO YOU TO REMIND YOURSELF OF ALL THE REASONS WHY YOU CAN AND WILL. OPTIMISM AND PESSIMISM ARE BOTH CHOICES. NOTICE THAT SOME OF THE MOST INTERESTING AND SUCCESSFUL PEOPLE HAVE CHOSEN TO ACQUIRE THE HABIT OF TALKING ABOUT WHAT THEY ARE FOR RATHER THAN WHAT THEY ARE AGAINST. BE ONE. **"I REALIZE THAT IDEALISM IS OUT OF SYNC WITH THE CYNICISM OF OUR AGE. SKEPTICISM HAS COME TO BE SYNONYMOUS WITH SOPHISTICATION, AND GLIBNESS IS MISTAKEN FOR INTELLIGENCE. IN SUCH AN ATMOSPHERE, WHY BOTHER AIMING HIGH? FAR TOO MANY PEOPLE DON'T. I JUST WANT TO REASSURE PEOPLE TO HAVE THE COURAGE TO PERSEVERE, TO KEEP FOLLOWING THEIR HEARTS EVEN WHEN OTHERS SCOFF. DON'T BE BEATEN DOWN BY NAYSAYERS. DON'T LET THE ODDS SCARE YOU FROM EVEN TRYING." —HOWARD SCHULTZ, CEO, STARBUCKS COFFEE CO**

Listen to the MUSTN'TS,
child,
listen to the don'ts—
listen to the shouldn'ts,
the impossibles,
the wont's—
listen to the never haves,
Then listen close to me.
Anything can happen,
child.
ANYTHING can be.

—Shel Silverstein

There's a silent killer that stalks America. It's called "rustout" and it's far more deadly and scary than burnout. Sure, burnout can wear down your body, but rustout can wipe out your soul and your spirit.

"Rustout is the slow death that follows when we stop making the choices that keep life alive. It's the feeling of numbness that comes from always taking the safe way, never accepting new challenges, continually surrendering to the day-to-day routine. Rustout means we are no longer growing, but at best, are simply maintaining. It implies that we have traded the sensation of life for the security of a paycheck... Rustout is the opposite of burnout. Burnout is overdoing. Rustout is underbeing."

Richard Leider and Steve Buchhoz, *The Rustout Syndrome*

Write down a few ways you can go stretch yourself for a good cause in the coming months:

Life is not a journey to the grave, with the goal of arriving safely and insignificantly at the end. Jump out of that rut. Leave your comfort zone. Go stretch yourself for a good cause. Don't just write to your state senator—take a whole scout troop to see him. Don't just watch NBA millionaires playing basketball on TV—go coach some inner-city kids at your local Boys or Girls Club. Don't just throw a buck or two in the Salvation Army kettle—throw on a Santa suit and go out and ring the bell yourself. This is your life, your one and only life. Don't keep a beautiful thing like that all to yourself. The very best thing you can do with your life is to give it away.

Go out and make a difference in your community. You don't need endless time and perfect conditions. Do it now. Do it today. Do it for twenty minutes and watch your heart start beating.
~Barbara Sher

of that rut!

If you want to make the days in your life really matter, then you must love s
good. *Victoria Wolff* Any journey in life—if not done for human reasons with un
sentiments in the world weigh less than a single lovely action. *James Russell Lo*
Robert Browning Things are beautiful if you love them. *Jean Anouilh* Work is love
love becomes our world. *Unknown* We know things better through love than th
a trembling happiness. *Anonymous* Life is the first gift, love is second, and und
the verb *to love...to help* is the most beautiful verb in the world. *Bertha von Suttr*
it is impossible to love without giving. *Richard Braunstein* There is only one path
We are shaped and fashioned by what we love. *Johann Wolfgang von Goethe* Life i
there. *Unknown* Where you find love, you find life. *Kobi Yamada* If you love wh
fundamental energy that nourishes us. It is our birthright. *Benjamin Shield* Lo
ness in thinking creates profoundness; kindness in giving creates love. *Lao-T*
déric Amiel Love wholeheartedly, be surprised, give thanks and praise—then
ing I believe that we're here to contribute love to the planet—each of us in ou
there are no impossibilities. *János Arany* If you judge people, you have no time
understand, I understand only because I love. *Leo Tolstoy* Love is enough. *Willi*
Live simply; love lavishly. *Michael Nolan* All works of love are works of peace.
but love. *William Sloane Coffin* What's so funny about peace, love and understa
up the stairs that love has built and looks out the windows which hope has o
that loves is always young. *Greek proverb* Do all things with love. *Og Mandino* L
is more potent than love? *Igor Stravinsky* Love is not what you are, but what yo
Hubbard If a thing loves, it is infinite. *William Blake* If you miss love, you miss l
Mother Teresa Understanding and love go together. *Jacob Needleman* And in the
We're here only to teach love. When we're doing that, our souls are singing a
a day's work, the sky. But nothing will save us. We were never meant to be sa
One heart. Let's get together and feel all right. *Bob Marley* In the end, the meas
love everywhere you go. *Mother Teresa* Life is short. Be swift with love! *Henri F*
bridge. *E.K. Donnelly* Love conquers all things; let us too surrender to love. *Virg*
a way. *English proverb* We remember best what we love most. *James Langdon* Lov
Robbins Talk to me like I'm someone you love. *Helen Hunt* I wish I woulda know
The whole worth of a kind deed lies in the love that inspires it. *Talmud* Love is
thy love; Love thy choice. *German proverb* It is a beautiful necessity of our nat
is a verb, if kindness is a verb, then you can do something about it. *Betty Eadie*
more; eat less, chew more; whine less, breathe more; talk less, say more; hate
Nin What the world really needs is more love and less paper work. *Pearl Baile*

bi Yamada All you need is love. *John Lennon* Love, genuine love, makes people and love—would be a very empty and lonely one. *Linda Blayne* All the beautiful ere is love there is life. *Mahatma Gandhi* Take away love and our earth is a tomb. *Khalil Gibran* We can only learn to love by loving. *Iris Murdoch* Any place that we edge. *Umberto Eco* Love is the greatest refreshment in life. *Pablo Picasso* Love is iird. *Marge Piercy* Regardless of the question, love is the answer. *Unknown* After love and do what you like. *St. Augustine* It is possible to give without loving, but n earth, we call it love. *Karen Goldman* To be loved, love. *Decimus Magnus Ausonius* comes only through great love. *Elbert Hubbard* Just keep putting your love out 1 will never work another day in your life. *Confucius* Love is our essence—the as strong as life. *Joseph Campbell* Kindness in words creates confidence; kind- e light. Forward is the motion. *Unknown* Hope is only the love of life. *Henri Fré-* ver the fullness of your life. *Brother David Steindl-Rast* Love is best. *Robert Brown-* rnie Siegel Only love makes life meaningful. *Anonymous* In dreams and in love, 1. *Mother Teresa* Do you love everybody you love? *Kobi Yamada* All, everything I e is the key to life, and its influences are those that move the world. *Ralph Trine* The world is too dangerous for anything but truth and too small for anything Costello To me life has meaning because we love. *Eleanor Roosevelt* Faith goes s Spurgeon Any time that is not spent on love is wasted. *Torquato Tasso* A heart atest gift that one generation can leave to another. *Richard Garnett* What force 1e. *Miguel de Cervantes* Life in abundance comes only through great love. *Elbert* glia What can you do to promote world peace? Go home and love your family. you take is equal to the love you make. *The Beatles* Love really is the answer. *Gerald Jampolsky* I think everything has value, absolute value, a child, a house, ere we meant for then? To love the whole damned world. *Jane Rule* One love. es will be the sum total of the love that we shared. *Benjamin Shield* Spread your verybody in the world wants to be loved—everybody. *Maya Angelou* Love is the e divided endlessly and still not diminish. *Anne Lindbergh* Love will always find the world. *Carter Heyward* Love is the single most important aspect of life. *John* ople. If I woulda knowed more, I woulda loved more. *Toni Morrison, from* Beloved s kind. It does not envy, it does not boast, it is not proud. *1 Corinthians 13:4* Choose mething. *Douglas Jerrold* If love is truly a verb, if help is a verb, if forgiveness love anything is to realize that it might be lost. *G.K. Chesterton* Fear less, hope re; and all good things are yours. *proverb* What I cannot love, I overlook. *Anaïs* ay love, but love? *Delariviere Manley* There is no place love is not. *Hugh Prather*

In Frank Capra's beloved Christmas movie, "It's a Wonderful Life," a penniless George Bailey (played by Jimmy Stewart) dies, believing that he was a failure. But a big-hearted angel named Clarence wisely allows George to go back in time and see how the lives of his friends and family would have been so much less had he not lived.

George Bailey's bank account may have been small, but he was a rich man. He quietly devoted a lifetime to being a loving husband and father, a caring neighbor and a loyal friend. "Remember, George: no man is a failure who has friends," says Clarence.

Seeing this for the first time in all its beauty and simplicity, George implores his angel, "Help me, Clarence, please, I want to live again!"

Strange, isn't it George? Each man's life touches so many other lives. When he isn't around he leaves an awful hole, doesn't he?
~Clarence the Angel, *It's a Wonderful Life*

erful Life

Belgian poet Maurice Maeterlinck once asked:

If you knew that you were going to die tonight, or merely that you would have to go away and never return, would you, looking upon family and friends for the last time, see them in the same light that you have previously seen them? Would you not love as you never yet have loved?

If you love someone, hurry up and show it. ~Rosie Zadra

IF YOU HAVE FAMILY OR FRIENDS TO FORGIVE, FORGIVE THEM NOW.

✳ IF YOU HAVE CHILDHOOD MEMORIES WORTH SAVORING OR CHILDHOOD

FRIENDS WORTH CALLING, CALL THEM NOW. ✳ IF YOUR MOTHER,

FATHER, SISTER OR BROTHER IS/ARE STILL LIVING, START A FRESH NEW

RELATIONSHIP WITH THEM NOW. ✳ IF SOMEONE ALREADY DIED BEFORE

YOU COULD TELL THEM WHAT YOU WANTED TO TELL THEM…GO AHEAD

AND TELL THEM NOW. ✳ IF THERE ARE CHILDREN (OR NIECES OR

NEPHEWS) IN YOUR LIFE, GIVE THEM THE POSITIVE EXPERIENCES THAT

YOU MAY HAVE MISSED AS A CHILD—AND DO IT NOW. ✳ IF YOU HAVE

A DREAM THAT IS CALLING YOU TO THE HEIGHTS, FOLLOW IT NOW. ✳

There are only so many tomorrows

IF YOU HAVE SPECIAL TALENTS, GIFTS, ABILITIES OR ENERGIES TO GIVE,

GIVE THEM NOW. ✳ IF THERE'S A CAUSE IN YOUR COMMUNITY WORTH

STANDING FOR—OR A BATTLE WORTH FIGHTING FOR—FIGHT FOR IT

NOW. ✳ IF YOU CAN HELP MAKE SOMEONE ELSE'S DREAM COME

TRUE, HELP IT COME TRUE NOW. ✳ IF THERE IS SOME KINDNESS

YOU CAN SHOW TO THE PEOPLE AROUND YOU, SHOW IT NOW. ✳

We are not living in eternity. We have only this moment, sparkling like a star in our hand, and melting like a snowflake.

~MARIE BEYON RAY

The great lesson...is that the sacred is *in* the ordinary, that it is to be found in one's daily life, in one's neighbors, friends, and family, in one's back yard.

~Abraham Maslow

If you have even one close friend in life, you are blessed.

WHO CAN EXPLAIN WHAT IT MEANS TO HAVE A FRIEND? SOMEONE WHO KNOWS YOU. SOMEONE WHO CARES. SOMEONE WHO LISTENS, OR REACHES OUT A HAND, OR HELPS YOU RALLY FROM DEFEAT. SOMEONE WHO'S GLAD YOU DROPPED BY. SOMEONE WHO WILL STAND BY YOU. A WELCOMING SMILE ACROSS THE ROOM. A BEAR HUG. SHARED STORIES, SHARED LAUGHTER, SHARED HOPES AND DREAMS, SHARED LIFE AND SHARED LOSS. THE WORLD IS A FAR SAFER, BRIGHTER PLACE WITH YOUR FRIEND IN IT. WHAT DOES IT MEAN TO HAVE A FRIEND? SIMPLY EVERYTHING.

The best way to keep a friend? Be one.

ONE OF YOUR FRIENDS MAY BE HURTING, DOUBTING, WONDERING OR STRUGGLING. ONE OF THEM MAY BE MISSING YOU. TONIGHT OR TOMORROW, PICK UP THE PHONE AND TELL THEM YOU CARE ABOUT THEM. TELL THEM YOU MISS THEM; OR TELL THEM YOU'RE SORRY. ARRANGE A VISIT. MAKE SOME TEA OR COFFEE, OR ENJOY A GLASS OF WINE. TAKE A WALK OR GO FOR A RUN TOGETHER. ENJOY THE SUN. EAT A POPSICLE. FEED THE BIRDS. LAUGH, HUG, CRY, REMINISCE. YOU ARE BOTH BLESSED.

The nudge

Every day we all have chance encounters with strangers, passing conversations with neighbors and routine contacts with our friends, colleagues or customers. If you think they don't matter, consider this:

A ball placed at the crest of a hill might roll into several different valleys depending on slight differences in initial position…or simply by an unexpected bump or "nudge" along the route.

It's the same in life. You don't have to be a "person of influence" to be influential. If you think back on your own life, it's very likely that some of the most influential people in your world may not even be aware of the things they taught you, or the direction they moved you.

Sometimes a patient, loving, well-intentioned minute from a busy but caring person can translate into a magnificent life-changing nudge for someone else. You have that power—use it.

If someone listens, or stretches out a hand, or whispers a kind word of encouragement, or attempts to understand, extraordinary things begin to happen. ~Loretta Gizartis

List some people who gave you a nudge—who had a significant influence on you, but probably didn't know it:

_____

_____

_____

_____

How will you thank them:

_____

_____

_____

_____

How will you intentionally nudge others:

_____

_____

_____

_____

What People Need is a Good Listening to

Henry David Thoreau mused that one of the greatest miracles would be if we could actually look through each other's eyes for an instant. Ironically, the best way to see the world through each other's eyes may be with our ears—by listening, really listening to each other.

Listening is not just etiquette; it's a way of loving, honoring and respecting. It's a way of bonding and connecting. It's a way of sharing ourselves and our humanity.

Ways to listen with compassion, understanding and intention:

Be present and give the speaker your full attention.

Show interest, be generous, encourage the speaker.

Listen with your heart as well as your ears.

Make it safe for the speaker to share his or her thoughts and feelings.

Listen to every word without interrupting or wishing to speak yourself.

When the speaker has finished, acknowledge what you heard without judging or correcting.

I felt it shelter to speak to you.
~Emily Dickinson

My theory is that everyone at one time
or another has been at the fringe of
society in some way: an outcast
in high school, a stranger in
a foreign country, the best
at something, the worst
at something, the one
who's different.
Being an out-
sider is the one
thing we all
have in
common.

~Alice Hoffman

How Big is Your Circle of Compassion?

Perfect compassion would be an all-encompasing circle with no center and no circumference. Visualize and list the people and things you love and care about in your circle. Now list some people or categories (groups, colors, ethnicities, etc.) not currently included in your circle. **How will you bring them in?**

WHAT CAN ONE DO?

The forest was quiet—too quiet. From out of nowhere came the clatter of horses' hooves, and then silence again. A few moments later a flame sprang from the dry leaves.

"Fire!" roared the bear. "Run for your lives," cried the crow. The forest animals, great and small, all fled in panic toward the river. But one small bird remained on the far bank watching the forest burn. "What can we do?" he cried out. There was no answer. "But this is our home," he cried again, "We must do something—it's on fire!" Silence was the only answer.

At last, he swooped down from his perch, scooped up a bill-full of water and flew over to dump it on the fire. Time after time he flew from the river to the fire until his weary wings were singed and covered with ash. High above, the gods looked down at the chaos below, and they laughed.

"What in the world is that little bird doing?" asked one god. "He is trying to put out the fire with a bill-full of water! But why? I will find out." And the god went down to Earth to ask the bird.

Later, when the god returned to the skies, he was surrounded by the other gods. "Well? What is he doing?" they all asked at once. The god replied softly, "He told me, 'I am but one. I cannot do everything, but I can do something.'"

Tears welled up in the gods' eyes and fell as gentle rain on the flames below, quenching the fire.

DO WHAT YOU CAN?

WHAT YOU CAN.

WHAT CAN YOU DO?

DO WHAT YOU CAN.

What will you use for your wake-up call?

You are, by accident of fate, alive at an absolutely critical moment in the history of our planet. Anything else you're interested in is not going to happen if you can't breathe the air and drink the water. Don't sit this one out. Do something. ~Carl Sagan

LOVE THE GREEN EARTH

The Power of One
It takes each of us to make a difference for all of us.

If everyone in the U.S. reused a paper grocery bag, even for just one shopping trip this year, we'd save millions of trees.

If everyone recycled just one additional plastic bottle this year, we'd reduce the plastic in our landfills by 200 million pounds.

If each of us simply kept our tires properly inflated this year, nationwide gasoline use would drop by millions of barrels.

If every American home replaced just one old-style light bulb with a compact fluorescent bulb, that would be like taking a million cars off the road for a year.

If every American paid his or her bills online instead of by mail, we'd save 16.5 million trees and eliminate the equivalent of 56,000 garbage trucks full of solid waste.

If each of us simply turned our water heaters down to 120°F, we would prevent millions of tons of CO_2 emissions per year.

If each of us simply reduced our computer default margin to .75" on all sides of our documents, we would save 6 million trees and eliminate 1.5 billion pounds of greenhouse gases per year.

When you're confronted with a problem, don't get down— get excited, get involved. A problem is an opportunity to do something generous or positive for the world. ~Heidi Wills

GREEN IS MANY THINGS: It is respect for the Earth and our place in it. It's a sense of wonder for the world around us. It's realizing that everything is connected. It's saying no to the status quo and yes to creating possibilities. It's giving our children's children something to work with. It's reverence for life. It is preserving and protecting what cannot be replaced. It's enjoying the world gently and living with good intention. GREEN IS a thousand conscious choices every day. It's not just a philosophy, it's a commitment and a way of life. It is being part of the solution. It's getting more out of life but taking less. It's pulling together with our community, our country and our world. It's knowing that the countless little things you do today will matter tomorrow. GREEN IS rising to the occasion. It is facing big challenges with even bigger ideas. It is turning "What if...?" into "We will...." "It is sustainability and caring about a future world you may never see. It is knowing in your heart that what you do does makes a difference. It is hope, it is action, it is positive change. GREEN IS caring about the world we live in—not just for today, but for tomorrow. It's looking at the future with fresh eyes, an open mind and a willing heart. It's thoroughly analyzing the way we've always done things and finding better ways of doing them. It is spirited debate and concerted action. It's standing up for what's right and setting a good example. It's quite possibly our last opportunity to restore the world and remake the future.

green is good.

WHERE DO YOU DRAW THE LINE BETWEEN POSSIBLE AND IMPOSSIBLE?

A teacher in his early thirties has earned the attention of 11,000 international global warming experts by doing something previously deemed virtually "impossible" with current technology.

When Louis Palmer heard that scientists around the world were looking for ways to reduce emissions of heat-trapping gases by 20 percent over the next few years, Palmer said, "We're aiming too low. I want to show that we can reduce emissions by 100 percent—that's what our world needs for the future."

So Palmer became a man with a mission. He took a leave of absence from his teaching job and, with help from Swiss engineers, built a 100 percent solar-powered two-seater car that travels up to 55 mph and covers 185 miles on a fully-charged battery.

To show people that the impossible was both possible and practical, he then spent 17 months driving his car around the world, traveling through 38 countries for a total of 32,000 miles—all without using a single drop of oil or gas.

Palmer's remarkable journey has already had an impact on thousands of delegates to the U.N. Climate Treaty Conference, as well as on major car-makers. Palmer says there's no reason why car companies couldn't make a much better version of his solar-powered car if they truly collaborated and set their minds to it.

"We have to stop saying it's impossible," he says. "These new technologies are ready. It's ecological, it's economical, it is absolutely reliable. We can stop global warming." We can, if we will.

Never tell a young person that something cannot be done. God may have waited centuries for someone ignorant enough of the impossible to do that very thing.

~John Andrew Holmes

ALL YOUR LIFE YOU ARE TOLD
THE THINGS YOU CANNOT DO.
ALL YOUR LIFE THEY WILL SAY
YOU'RE NOT GOOD ENOUGH OR STRONG
ENOUGH OR TALENTED ENOUGH,
THEY'LL SAY YOU'RE THE WRONG
HEIGHT OR THE WRONG WEIGHT
OR THE WRONG TYPE TO PLAY
THIS OR BE THIS OR ACHIEVE THIS.
THEY WILL TELL YOU NO,
A THOUSAND TIMES NO UNTIL ALL THE
NO'S BECOME MEANINGLESS.
ALL YOUR LIFE THEY WILL TELL YOU NO,
QUITE FIRMLY AND VERY QUICKLY.
THEY WILL TELL YOU NO. AND
YOU WILL TELL THEM YES.

~NIKE ADVERTISEMENT

motto

We forget sometimes that Americans are descended from revolutionaries and rebels—people who dared to dissent from British rule. This nation was born when a small band of patriots got mad enough to sign the Declaration of Independence. Getting mad in a constructive way is an American tradition that is good for our souls, good for everyone.

It was Ben Franklin who chose the motto on our dollar bill—*Annuit Coeptis*—which basically means that God favors bold enterprises.

"E Pluribus Unum" is another famous motto. It appears on our national seal, and it means "one from many." It's a guiding principle not only for our democracy, but for thousands of large and small non-profit organizations that derive their power from individuals banding together for a common cause.

Put it all together and you have a good description of community service: Small groups of caring citizens boldly upsetting our apple cart with new ways to improve the world around us.

What's the guiding principle or motto for *your* movement?

If you don't have one yet, why not write one today. "Throw the tea overboard" is already taken, but here's some inspiration to get you going:

Imagine life without breast cancer.
Susan G. Komen motto

The greatest tragedy is indifference.
Red Cross motto

Every individual has a role to play.
Jane Goodall Institute motto

Take down the tiger trade.
Humane Gifts

Do good in the hood.
Do Good in the Hood

Conserve the Earth's living heritage.
Conservation International

Church with its sleeves rolled up.
Auckland Community Churches

Think globally, eat locally.
Harvest International

Cancer doesn't sleep and neither do we.
Relay for Life

Speak up for the sharks.
Ocean Conservancy

Saving backyard animal habitats.
Ernie McLaney's One Man Blog

Share the power of a wish with a child.
Make-a-Wish Foundation

Accelerate practical and profitable solutions to global warming.
Climate Solutions

Life in all its fullness for every child.
World Vision

Something can be done about it.
Boston Volunteer Mission

Go ahead and make my day.
Seniors Serving Seniors

My motto is:

_____

_____

_____

The Arithmetic of
Making a Difference

Service to others has its own arithmetic. Combine two or more good-hearted people in the pursuit of a common cause, and suddenly one-plus-one is more than two. It's called synergy. We can all do a little something, but together we can do something truly amazing.

If we all use the arithmetic of service, there isn't a problem in this world that can't be solved. The hard part is convincing each person that they play a significant part in the equation—that each of us has something to give which cannot otherwise be given—that we all contribute a very critical factor in the multiplier effect.

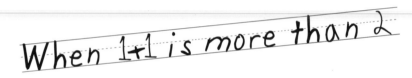

When 1+1 is more than 2

5 Hours a Week: Using the arithmetic of service one person could change the social landscape of our country in a few hours a week. How? If every American donated just five hours a week to a good cause, it would equal the labor of 20 million full-time volunteers.

4 Hours a Month: If every employee in every American company were given just four hours a month to volunteer for a cause of their choice, American companies could transform thousands of neighborhoods and millions of lives.

A Few Minutes a Day: In her book, *The Difference a Day Makes,* Karen Jones lists hundreds of small, empowering acts of humanity that anyone can work into their day. Shop at the farmer's market. Take a neighbor's dog for a walk. Take your old magazines to the senior center on the way to work. If we all did just one small action each day, we'd create an army of everyday altruists.

Bridging the Gap

In 1855, the great Niagara Suspension Bridge was built by flying a child's kite across the 855-foot chasm. Attached to the kite was a string, attached to the string was a cord, attached to the cord was a rope, and attached to the rope was a cable—sure and strong.

Our world needs more kite-flyers and bridge-builders. If you have a big idea or a project in mind, step one is to take step one. Just fly your kite to the other side and go from there. Big positive changes are seldom accomplished all at once; it's usually a matter of one step leading to another. What are you waiting for?

If you don't like the way the world is, you change it. You have an obligation to change it. You just do it one step at a time.

—Marian Wright Edelman

Go fly a kite:

1) My big project is:

_____

_____

_____

2) My first step will be:

_____

_____

_____

3) My target date for the first step is:

_____

_____

_____

THE MAN IN THE METRO: IT WAS ALL VIDEOTAPED BY A HIDDEN CAMERA. HE WAS A YOUNG WHITE MAN IN JEANS, T-SHIRT AND A WASHINGTON NATIONALS BASEBALL CAP. HE POSITIONED HIMSELF BY A TRASH BASKET AT A METRO STATION IN WASHINGTON, D.C. AND STARTED TO PLAY THE VIOLIN FOR PASSING PEDESTRIANS. HE PLAYED SIX BACH PIECES DURING THE RUSH HOUR AS THOUSANDS OF PEOPLE FILED THROUGH THE STATION, MOST OF THEM ON THEIR WAY TO WORK. AFTER THE FIRST FOUR MINUTES WENT BY, A MAN BRIEFLY LEANED AGAINST THE WALL TO LISTEN BUT THEN LOOKED AT HIS WATCH AND STARTED TO WALK AGAIN, CLEARLY LATE FOR WORK. A LITTLE LATER THE VIOLINIST RECEIVED A DOLLAR TIP FROM A WOMAN WHO TOSSED THE MONEY IN HIS OPEN VIOLIN CASE, BUT WITHOUT STOPPING. OTHERS FLIPPED IN QUARTERS, NICKELS OR PENNIES ON THE RUN. THE ONES WHO PAID THE MOST ATTENTION WERE THE CHILDREN. THE WASHINGTON POST REPORTED, "EVERY SINGLE TIME A CHILD WALKED PAST, HE OR SHE TRIED TO STOP AND WATCH. AND EVERY SINGLE TIME, A PARENT SCOOTED THE KID AWAY." IN THE 45 MINUTES THE MUSICIAN PLAYED, ONLY SIX PEOPLE STOPPED AND STAYED FOR A WHILE. OTHERS WHO WERE ON THEIR CELL PHONES SPOKE LOUDER AS THEY PASSED THE VIOLINIST, SO THEIR VOICES COULD BE HEARD OVER THE MUSIC. WHEN HE FINISHED PLAYING AND SILENCE TOOK OVER, NO ONE NOTICED AND NO ONE APPLAUDED. NO ONE KNEW THAT THE VIOLINIST WAS ACTUALLY JOSHUA BELL, THE INTERNATIONALLY ACCLAIMED VIRTUOSO. THAT DAY IN THE METRO HE PLAYED ONE OF THE GREATEST PIECES OF MUSIC EVER WRITTEN—BACH'S PARTITA NO. 2—ON A STRADIVARIUS WORTH $3.5 MILLION. JUST TWO DAYS BEFORE, HE HAD SOLD OUT A THEATER IN BOSTON WHERE THE TICKETS AVERAGED $100. LIFE'S MUSIC IS EVERYWHERE AND ALL AROUND US. IF WE DO NOT HAVE A MOMENT TO STOP AND LISTEN TO ONE OF THE BEST MUSICIANS IN THE WORLD PLAYING SOME OF THE BEST MUSIC EVER WRITTEN, HOW MANY OTHER THINGS ARE WE MISSING?

What is this life if, full of care, We have no time to stand and stare. —W.H. Davies

What It's Like to Be Reborn

By Vickie Girard, Stage IV Cancer Survivor

We cancer patients receive a unique gift. Yes, we know what it's like to come too close to death, but we also know what it's like to be reborn. I remember vividly the day I first stepped outside the hospital—released at last from weeks of undergoing a bone marrow transplant. Oh, if that wonderful rush of the senses could be bottled, it would be worth a thousand times its weight in gold.

It was a beautiful summer day, but beautiful is inadequate. The colors that day were turned up, as if I had been seeing with poor reception before. The scents in the air were almost overpowering. I could smell fresh-cut grass, growing flowers, traffic, food—I could smell the time of day. Morning smells different than evening or midday.

The sounds rushed at me. Voices, no longer filtered or contained by hospital walls, had a different ring outside. I heard a dog bark, a horn honk, a child yell, shoes hitting pavement, and multiple conversations going on all around me. And the feeling—there was a slight breeze and I could feel my skin. It was almost as if the air itself had texture as it touched my face and arms. The sun, it warmed me from the outside in. Even walking felt different than it had in hospital corridors.

Had the world always been like this, this alive? I vowed to always look at life this way, to never forget this moment.

How will you give something

beautiful
to the
world?

...the tragedy in life does not lie in not reaching your goal. The tragedy lies in having no goal to reach. It isn't a calamity to die with dreams unfulfilled, but it is a calamity not to dream. It is not a disaster to be unable to capture your ideal, but it is a disaster to have no ideal to capture. It is not a disgrace not to reach the stars, but it is a disgrace to have no stars to reach for. ~Benjamin E. Mays

The Story of Bernard Lown:
One Man's Journey to End Nuclear Weapons

Bernard Lown, the good-hearted Physician Emeritus at Harvard Medical School, is best known as the inventor of the heart defibrillator—a remarkable device that has "shocked" literally millions of hearts back to life over the past 50 years.

But there's another, far-greater quest in Dr. Lown's life. Together with his Russian counterpart, Dr. Evgueni Chazov, they set out to face down the worldwide threat of nuclear war on behalf of all mankind. In 1986, they were awarded the Nobel Peace Prize for establishing the International Physicians for the Prevention of War.

Against all odds they grew the organization to more than 150,000 physicians. Together those physicians were able to gather enough data to prove to world leaders that our planet could not survive a nuclear war. There wouldn't be enough physicians and hospitals to care for those who might survive, and all humanity would die.

In his late eighties, Dr. Lown still travels throughout the world, urging everyday individuals not to be intimidated about taking on global issues on their own. He reminds all of us: "Some of life's biggest and most positive changes are propelled by mini conspiracies of a few well-meaning folks."

Never doubt that a small group of thoughtful, committed citizens can change the world; indeed, it is the only thing that ever has. ~Margaret Mead

May peace and peace an

eace be everywhere. ~The Upanishads

For 31 years Erma Bombeck wrote more than 4,000 hilarious newspaper columns chronicling the everyday life of a suburban housewife and her kids. She used to say, "When I stand before God at the end of my life, I would hope that I would not have a single bit of talent left, and could say, 'I used everything you gave me.'"

In her columns and books, Erma would pretend to tear her hair out over frustration

THE WISDOM OF CHILDREN

with her children. "My kids refuse to eat anything that hasn't danced on TV," she once wrote.

She also said, "Never loan your car to anyone to whom you've given birth." And perhaps her most famous quote: "Insanity is hereditary—you get it from your kids." In real life, however, Erma spoke almost reverently about the "wisdom of children" and the importance that all of us should place on maintaining a child's outlook on life until the day we die. "I talked with mothers who had lost a child to cancer," wrote Erma. "Every single one said that death gave their lives new meaning and purpose. And who do you think prepared these mothers for the rough, lonely road they had to travel? Their dying child. It was the children who pointed their mothers toward the future and told them to keep going."

If children with terminal cancer can find love, joy, beauty and peace in their day—and they do— why don't we? —*Dan Zadra*

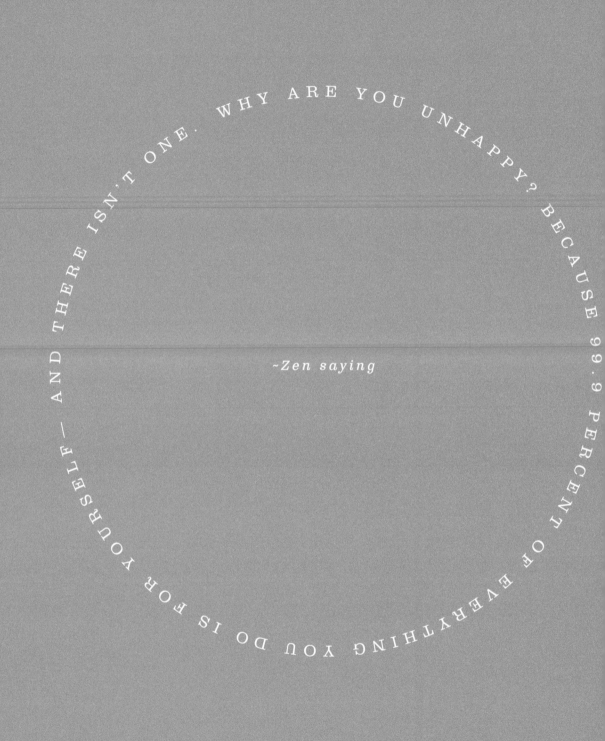

WHY ARE YOU UNHAPPY? BECAUSE 99.9 PERCENT OF EVERYTHING YOU DO IS FOR YOURSELF— AND THERE ISN'T ONE.

~Zen saying

Rabbi Harold Kushner famously said, "The happiest people I know are people who don't even think about being happy. They just think about being good neighbors, good people. And then happiness sort of sneaks in the back window while they are busy doing good."

Who are the five happiest people I know?

_____

_____

_____

_____

_____

What kinds of things are they doing for others?

_____

_____

_____

_____

Two Wolves

A Cherokee elder was teaching his children about life.

He said to them, "A terrible fight is going on inside me.

It is a fight between two wolves. One is the wolf of joy,

love, hope, kindness and compassion. The other is the

wolf of fear, anger, cynicism, indifference and greed.

The same fight is going on inside of you and every other

person too." The children thought about it for a moment,

and then one child asked, "Which wolf will win?" The elder

replied, "Whichever one you feed."

Life is either a daring adventure or nothing at all. *Helen Keller*

Life is a song. Love is the music. *Cindy Vail*

Life is a glass given to us to fill. *William Brown*

Life is a splendid gift. There is nothing small about it. *Florence Nightingale*

Life is not a problem to solve, it's a gift to cherish. *Don Ward*

Life is something to be in, not something to get through. *Dustin Hoffman*

Life is to be felt, not figured out. *Thomas Hardy*

Life is what we are alive to. It is not length but breadth. *Maltbie Babcock*

Life is a verb, not a noun. *Charlotte Gilman*

Life isn't all golf. *Tiger Woods*

Life is a chance to grow a soul. *A. Powell Davies*

Life is the childhood of eternity. *Johann Wolfgang von Goethe*

Life is but a day at most. *Robert Burns*

Life is what you make it. Always has been, always will be. *Grandma Moses*

What's your philosophy of life?

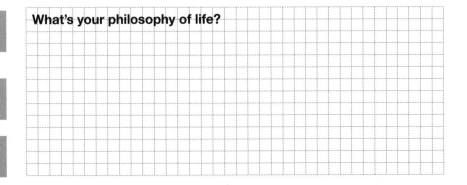

At the end of your life, you will never regret not having passed one more test, not winning one more verdict or not closing one more deal. You will regret time not spent with a husband, a child, a friend or a parent.

~Barbara Bush

All of the other shallow things will not matter. I won't have any money to leave behind. I won't have the fine and luxurious things of life to leave behind. But I want to leave a committed life behind.

~Martin Luther King, Jr.

When you die and go to heaven, our maker is not going to ask, "Why didn't you discover the cure for such and such?" The only question we will be asked in that precious moment is, "Why didn't you become you?"

~Elie Wiesel

The questions asked at the end of life are very simple ones: "Did I love well? Did I love the people around me, my community, the earth, in a deep way?" And perhaps, "Did I live fully? Did I offer myself to life?"

~Jack Kornfeld

The only thing you take with you when you're gone is what you leave behind.
WHAT WILL YOU LEAVE BEHIND?

Here is the
test to find
whether or not
your mission
on earth is
finished: If you
are alive, it isn't.
~Richard Bach

Years ago, Sam Levinson was filled with joy and hope at the birth of his new granddaughter. One night he sat down and wrote a letter to her—something he hoped she would read again and again as she grew up and made her way through the world. He wrote, in part, **"We leave you a tradition with a future. The tender loving care of human beings will never become obsolete. People, even more than things, have to be restored, renewed, revived, reclaimed, and redeemed and redeemed and redeemed. As you grow older you will discover that you have two hands—one for helping yourself and the other for helping others. Never throw anyone away."**

May God bless you with the foolishness to think that you can make a difference in the world, so that you will do the things which others tell you cannot be done. You have great days still ahead of you. May there be many of them.
~Unknown

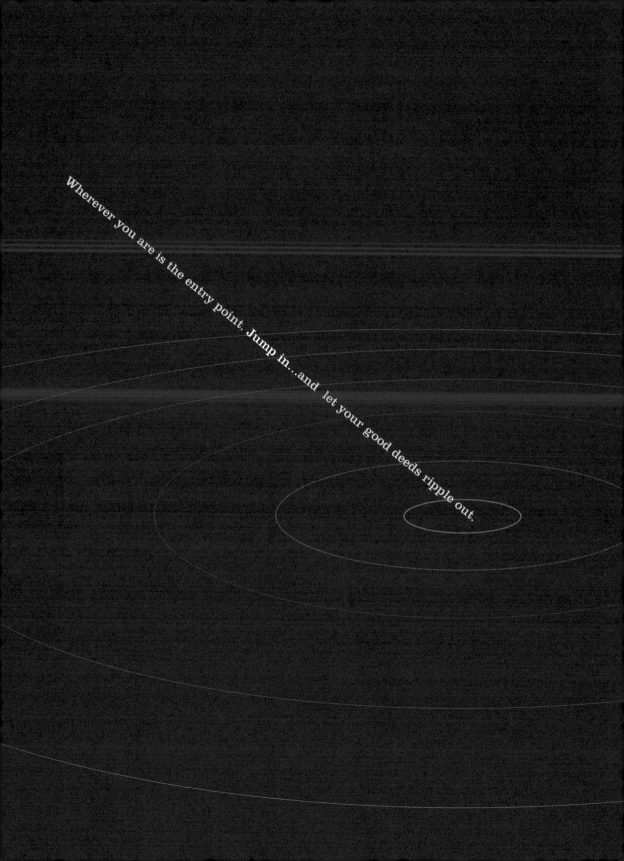

Wherever you are is the entry point. Jump in…and let your good deeds ripple out.